Let's Play Tag!

 Read the Page

 Read the Story

 Game

 Yes No

 Repeat

 Stop

INTERNET CONNECTION REQUIRED FOR AUDIO DOWNLOAD.

To use this book with the Tag™ Reader you must download audio from the LeapFrog® Connect Application.
The LeapFrog Connect Application can be installed from the CD provided with your Tag Reader or at leapfrog.com/tag.

WANTED: KEVIN LEVIN

WRITTEN BY *CHARLOTTE FULLERTON* • ART BY *MIN S. KU*
COLORS/COLOURS BY *HI-FI COLOUR DESIGN*

Forever Knights? Hold them off as best you can! We'll be right there!

I know a shortcut. Hang on!

SCREEEECH

Look! A shooting star!

Where?

I could've moved that for you, Kevin.

Mmhhh.

Kevin? Are you **OK**?

Nyahah.

As they *drive away*, a *mysterious figure* emerges from the *shadows*.

 וֹ בַם ؟

BRAIN STORM!

Have some of my *brain power!*

Kevin! What are you *doing* still *tinkering* with that thing?

Nff...

...gehh.

He's trying to capture *you*, Kevin! *Run! Duck! Do something!*

Hmm, the *bounty hunter* seems to have located his *quarry.*

Where did they go?

SevenSeven is a *bounty hunter.* And his quarry is *Kevin.*

That *could* mean Kevin is back to his old, *evil ways.*

I don't believe it! There *has* to be some other explanation.

I *don't want* to *believe* it either, Gwen. But you've got to *admit*, it looks *bad*.

When we *find* him, we'll ask *him*.

This thing Kevin was building, it's the last object he touched. I can use it to...

You *freak* me out sometimes, *Gwen*.

Found him! We've got to *get* to him *fast!*

Leave that to *me*.

SevenSeven and his prisoner, Kevin, have teleported to the woods near SevenSeven's spaceship.

Unghgh!

BOOM

Suddenly, a *sonic boom* blasts through the *air!*

I've got to figure out how to turn off those blasters outside!

It's got to be one of these buttons. But which one?

There we go!

Back outside the ship...

Must. Use. Device. Now.

Kevin grabs the alien tech device and uses it on...

...himself!

Ahhhhh!

An alien lifeform of pure energy flies out of Kevin!

What was that?

17